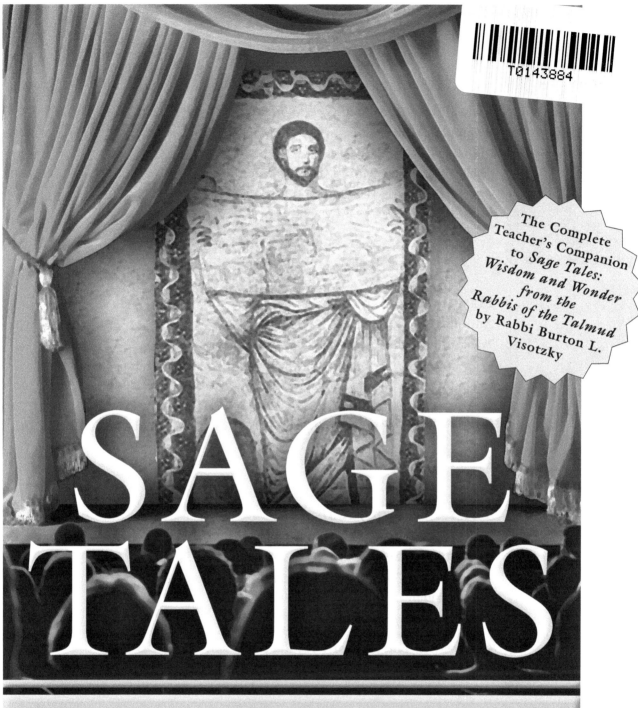

The Complete Teacher's Companion to *Sage Tales: Wisdom and Wonder from the Rabbis of the Talmud* by Rabbi Burton L. Visotzky

SAGE TALES

Wisdom and Wonder from the Rabbis of the Talmud

Teacher's Guide

Rabbi Burton L. Visotzky

Ethics of the Sages
Pirke Avot—Annotated & Explained

Translation & Annotation by Rabbi Rami Shapiro

Clarifies the ethical teachings of the early Rabbis and highlights parallels with other faith traditions.

5½ x 8½, 192 pp, Quality PB, 978-1-59473-207-2

A book from SkyLight Paths, Jewish Lights' sister imprint

Hasidic Tales
Annotated & Explained

Translation & Annotation by Rabbi Rami Shapiro

Brings the legendary tales of the impassioned Hasidic rabbis to life by presenting them as stories rather than as parables.

5½ x 8½, 240 pp, Quality PB, 978-1-893361-86-7

A book from SkyLight Paths, Jewish Lights' sister imprint

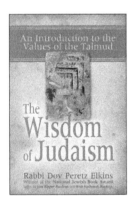

The Wisdom of Judaism
An Introduction to the Values of the Talmud

By Rabbi Dov Peretz Elkins

Accessible…. Contributes significantly to our practical understanding of Talmudic wisdom.

6 x 9, 192 pp, Quality PB, 978-1-58023-327-9

Also available: **The Wisdom of Judaism Teacher's Guide**

8½ x 11, 18 pp, PB, 978-1-58023-350-7

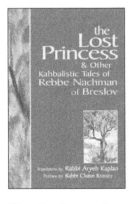 

The Lost Princess
& Other Kabbalistic Tales of Rebbe Nachman of Breslov

Translation by Rabbi Aryeh Kaplan; Preface by Rabbi Chaim Kramer

6 x 9, 400 pp, Quality PB, 978-1-58023-217-3

The Seven Beggars
& Other Kabbalistic Tales of Rebbe Nachman of Breslov

Translation by Rabbi Aryeh Kaplan; Preface by Rabbi Chaim Kramer

6 x 9, 192 pp, Quality PB, 978-1-58023-250-0

Captivating and entertaining stories that convey lessons about God and perceptions of the world around us. Presents Rebbe Nachman's beloved teachings accompanied by illuminating commentary drawn from the works of Rebbe Nachman's pupils.

SAGE TALES

Wisdom and Wonder from the Rabbis of the Talmud

Teacher's Guide

Rabbi Burton L. Visotzky

Contents

For People of All Faiths, All Backgrounds

JEWISH LIGHTS Publishing

Sage Tales: Wisdom and Wonder from the Rabbis of the Talmud Teacher's Guide

ISBN 978-1-58023-460-3 (pbk)
ISBN 978-1-68336-276-0 (hc)

Published by Jewish Lights Publishing
www.jewishlights.com

Introduction

Sage Tales: Wisdom and Wonder from the Rabbis of the Talmud is divided into twenty-two chapters. It is designed for a course offered twice weekly for a full semester, allowing for sessions for the course introduction and requirements, a mid-term, and an in-class final. In other words, it was written by an undergraduate professor for *undergraduate* or *master's* level faculty who wish to introduce their students to rabbinic narrative conventions and poetics.

Of course, these stories also teach moral lessons, which may be explored by *all* readers. *Sage Tales* is therefore also designed for use by *high schools* and *adult study* circles, *congregational study groups*, as well as *reading groups*.

Typically a *reading group* will read the entire book from one meeting to the next, and then join together for discussion. There is a readers' discussion guide (RDG) incorporated into this teacher's guide to help facilitate discussion. The RDG also will help adult study and high school educators key in on themes that run through the rabbinic narratives chosen for *Sage Tales*.

While there are twenty-two chapters (and you can use the headings to teach/learn the Hebrew alphabet), *the book may be broken into units for study over shorter periods.*

Lesson Plan

Here's a plan to teach *Sage Tales* in seven to nine lessons.

Lesson 1

Chapters 1 through 3 constitute a unit, introducing the rabbis who are the *founding fathers of Rabbinic Judaism*. They flourish before and immediately following the destruction by Roman troops of Jerusalem and its Temple in the year 70 CE.

Lesson 2

Chapters 4 and 5 are stories about the *death of children and theodicy* (explaining God's role when bad things happen to good people). These chapters may be skipped for high school classes. If they are included in the lesson plan, much as with adult groups, educators should be prepared for the possibility of strong emotional responses to the material.

Lesson 3

Chapters 6 and 7 tell the story of Rabbi Eliezer ben Hyrcanus and how he came to Torah. They may be joined together as a unit.

Lesson 4

Chapters 8 through 11 are a unit on early *rabbinic mysticism*.

Lesson 5

Chapters 12 through 15 cover the *destruction of Jerusalem during the war against Rome* (66–70 CE). These may be read together and studied with a focus on rabbinic responses to the fall of the Temple cult and the invention of rabbinic Judaism.

Lesson 6

Chapters 16 through 19 focus on rainmaker stories, with an interlude on Jesus in Talmudic literature. The *rainmaker stories*, as well as Chapter 19's *sleeper motif*, allow students to consider the role *folklore* takes in Jewish narrative. Students can be asked to compare and contrast the various motifs, or even make up their own folktales.

Lesson 7

Chapter 17 (Nicodemus and Buni—Uncensored!) might be taught separately as a lesson on *Judaism and Christianity* in their formative years. Themes to explore include censorship and the fraught history of the sister religions. Given the demographics of the American Jewish community, this might be a good place to discuss Jewish-Christian relations in general and within families in specific. It is also possible to gloss over this chapter.

Lesson 8

Chapters 20 and 21 similarly explore the *development of a legendary folk motif*—the poor little rich girl who has fallen from her wealth. Here, the unfolding of traditions over a long period, like a centuries-long game of "telephone," helps explain how stories evolve, sometimes even shifting the morals they teach.

Lesson 9

Chapter 22, which focuses on *Jerusalem*, is meant as a benediction to the entire collection of *Sage Tales*. In this chapter, Rabbi Visotzky alludes to the contested nature of Jerusalem as a Holy City for Judaism, Christianity, and Islam. This can give rise to discussion of modern issues such as Jewish-Muslim relations in general, and Israeli-Palestinian politics, in specific. Teachers need to be prepared for the possibility of heated debate if these topics are considered. To properly cover the interreligious and political issues, a separate course is recommended.

Supporting Material

To support this lesson plan, the book has the following resources:

- The complete texts in English, along with a listing of where to find the *original sources* in Hebrew and Aramaic. This way, the texts may be studied separately (first) from Rabbi Visotzky's explanations and commentary.
- A *glossary* of terms and places.
- A *who's who directory* of rabbis and other characters mentioned in the book.

Educators are encouraged to write the author at buvisotzky@jtsa.edu to discuss *Sage Tales* and how to present it.

Discussion Guide

Along with lesson plan outlined above, this discussion guide may also be used as a means of taking a thematic approach to the stories found in *Sage Tales*.

1. *Sage Tales* is a book about stories. The author makes it clear that he thinks they probably didn't happen the way they are told, if at all. What is the difference between history and story? Why might a good story be more truthful than a first-person account of an historic event?

2. Rabbinic literature was composed by men (rabbis) for men (more rabbis). How do these story tellers construct their ideas about *women*? Think about Beruriah (Rabbi Meir's bereaved wife), Martha bat Boethius, and the daughter of Nicodemus ben Gurion. What virtues do they share in common? How do they conform to our current notions of femininity?

3. While we are thinking of how the rabbis constructed an idea of what is feminine, how did they imagine masculinity? Are the rabbis "real men"? Think of Rabbi Meir, Rabbi Eliezer ben Hyrcanus, even Rabbi Yohanan ben Zakkai escaping from Jerusalem and confronting the general Vespasian. How do these men conform to your ideas of masculinity?

4. For the past number of years there has been a growing interest in spirituality and Jewish mysticism. Do the stories in this book, which talk about rabbis speculating on God's chariot or hearing Divine voices, paint a spiritual picture? How might you define mysticism for the rabbis of the Talmud? How does it differ from modern interest in Kabbalah and Jewish spirituality?

5. Two of the stories in this book are about the death of children. In ancient times, infant mortality was much higher than it is today. How have our means of coping with the death of children changed from the ways the ancient rabbis talked about parents' grieving?

6. The story of Martha bat Boethius was presented in this book as a Keystone-Kops type of comic relief to the tragic narrative of the destruction of Jerusalem. Yet one could argue that the Martha story is equally tragic, with her servant not being clownish but representing the increasing panic and despair at finding food during the siege. Martha, then, would be a potent symbol of defeat and desperation. Discuss this way of reading her place in the Talmudic story.

7. Rabbi Visotzky refers to Jesus, Christianity, the Prophet Muhammad, and Islam. Why do you think he does this in a book about rabbinic Judaism? What messages might he be trying to convey about the historical milieu in which these stories were first told? What message might he be trying to teach us for today?

8. Honi was a rainmaker (in the old fashioned sense of the term). He had a special relationship with God. Yet, it seems that the very relationship that gave him his mantic power left him arrogant and aloof from his fellows. In the end, he died a lonely old man. Discuss the value of community. Hint: Look around the room at the people with whom you are discussing and sharing this book. Hugging is permitted.

Rabbi Burton L. Visotzky has been engaging spiritual seekers with the ancient wisdom of Judaism for over forty years. He is Appleman Professor of Midrash and Interreligious Studies and director of the Louis Finkelstein Institute for Religious and Social Studies at The Jewish Theological Seminary of America. Dr. Visotzky consulted with Bill Moyers and was a featured participant in the PBS television series *Genesis: A Living Conversation.* He is a lecturer and scholar-in-residence in synagogues, churches and mosques throughout North America, and the author of nine other books, including *Reading the Book: Making the Bible a Timeless Text.*

Praise for *Sage Tales: The Wisdom and Wonder from the Rabbis of the Talmud*

"One of our tradition's liveliest teachers has managed to capture all of his rare vibrancy on the page. Who knew that Midrash could read like a great detective story?"
—**Abigail Pogrebin**, author, *Stars of David*

"Both ancient and timeless ... this retelling and retooling of ancient rabbinic wisdom tales [does] the sages and us a great service. Brings these ... sages alive that we might hear their wisdom once more. A book to be savored."
—**Rabbi Rami Shapiro**, author, *Hasidic Tales: Annotated and Explained*

"Lets you reach ... into the collective consciousness of Jewish value teachings and offers you a glimpse into what life ought to be and can be."
—**Reb Zalman Schachter-Shalomi**, author, *First Steps to a New Jewish Spirit*

"Wit, insight and deep sensitivity permeate every sentence and draw the reader into an irresistible journey to uncover the spiritual, intellectual and emotional underpinnings of rabbinic literature. [An] important contribution to the field."
—**Rabbi Sharon Brous**, IKAR

For People of All Faiths, All Backgrounds
JEWISH LIGHTS Publishing

www.jewishlights.com

 Find us on Facebook®
Facebook is a registered
trademark of Facebook, Inc.

Insights, Ideas and Thoughtful Questions for Discussing with Students the Wisdom Tales of the Ancient Rabbis

A helpful guide to creative use of *Sage Tales: The Wisdom and Wonder of the Rabbis of the Talmud* in the classroom. Includes:

- An overview of how to use *Sage Tales* in a variety of educational settings
- A lesson plan for how to teach *Sage Tales* in seven to nine sessions
- Intriguing discussion questions to guide students in an exploration of key themes found in the wisdom tales of the ancient rabbis

This teaching tool will help you guide each student to a deeper understanding of early rabbinic Judaism and the wise lessons hidden within the narratives of the rabbis of that time.

About *Sage Tales: The Wisdom and Wonder of the Rabbis of the Talmud*

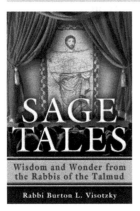

6 x 9, 256 pp, Hardcover
978-1-58023-456-6

Great stories have the power to draw the heart. But certain stories have the power to draw the heart to God and awaken the better angels of our nature. Such are the tales of the rabbis of the Talmud, colorful, quirky yarns that tug at our heartstrings and test our values, ethics, morality—and our imaginations.

In this collection for people of all faiths and backgrounds, Rabbi Burton Visotzky draws on four decades of telling and teaching these legends in order to unlock their wisdom for the contemporary heart. He introduces you to the cast of characters, explains their motivations, and provides the historical background needed to penetrate the wise lessons often hidden within these unusual narratives.

In learning how and why these oft-told tales were spun, you discover how they continue to hold value for our lives.

Praise for *Sage Tales: The Wisdom and Wonder of the Rabbis of the Talmud*

"Enlivens ancient wisdom with modern whimsy, decodes Talmudic enigmas with narrative grace, and humanizes the giants of early rabbinic Judaism in ways that make each character real, quirky and unforgettable. Has there ever been a book of solid scholarship that was this much fun to read?"

—**Letty Cottin Pogrebin**, author, *Deborah, Golda and Me: Being Female and Jewish in America*; founding editor, *Ms.* magazine

"A treasure trove of information, insight and meaning. It is a 'must read' for anyone interested in knowing more about rabbinic texts, traditions and history, while being charmed and entertained. Be prepared to experience rabbinic Judaism come alive!"

—**Dr. Norman Cohen**, author, *The Way Into Torah*

"A revelation…. A thrilling journey full of wisdom, humor and timeless lessons…. In short, Rabbi Visotzky has blessed us with a deep and lasting gift, a spectacular work that we want to read over and over again."

—**Rabbi Naomi Levy**, author, *Hope Will Find You* and *To Begin Again*

"Reading *Sage Tales* is like going to the best show on Broadway followed by an elegant dinner with a critic, a holy skeptic who is illuminating, entertaining, learned and enlightening…. I loved this book!"

—**Rabbi Irwin Kula**, author, *Yearnings: Embracing the Sacred Messiness of Life*; co-author, *The Book of Jewish Sacred Practices*

For People of All Faiths, All Backgrounds

JEWISH LIGHTS Publishing
www.jewishlights.com

Printed in the USA
CPSIA information can be obtained
at www.ICGtesting.com
JSHW060239160824
68134JS00058BA/2703

9 781580 234603